C000258404

The Heyday of the ROUTEMASTER

Celebrity Travel

Geoff Rixon

IAN ALLAN
Publishing

Front cover:

Change of Service

The demise of trolleybus route 604 on 8 May 1962 resulted in the extension of route 131 from Kingston to Wimbledon. Eight days later, brand-new RM1164 passes Biggs the Butchers in Walton Road, East Molesey. This vehicle later went to East Midland, who re-registered it as NSG 636A in 1989, before selling it to its current owners, Bluebird Buses of Perth. *Geoff Rixon*

Back cover:

Chance Meeting

Two of London's more unusual Routemasters run neck and neck around Marble Arch in October 1994. On the left is East London's re-registered RMC1456, one of three former Green Line coaches to be found on route 15. Nearer the camera is ER880, the designation given on delivery to the first extended Routemaster, but changed to RML880 before the bus entered service. This vehicle, which now has a Cummins engine, belongs to London United and wears the former tramway livery. *Geoff Rixon*

Title page:

Short-Lived Splendour

The rainbow colours of Celebrity Travel which adorned this Routemaster lasted only five months. Midway through its advertising contract in July 1973, RM294 waits at the Crystal Palace terminus of route 137 before returning to Highate. It ended its working life at Enfield. *R. C. Riley*

Left:

Wasted Effort

After RM2217, all the remainder of the class were long Routemasters and the first batch were 43 Green Line coaches. These were intended to replace the RTs on double-deck routes such as the 721, 722 and 723. RCL2228, seen here at Aldgate in June 1965, had just entered service. Within a few years it was relegated, like all the coach Routemasters, to green bus service and passed to London Country in 1970 when London Transport (LT) relinquished its Country Department. In 1980 the vehicle was re-acquired by LT and refurbished at considerable expense for operation on route 149, only to be scrapped four years later. *James Whiting*

Right:

Promenader

The garish backdrop of Blackpool's seafront provides a change of scene for RM879 which was purchased along with 11 other Leyland-engined Routemasters from London Buses in 1986 and 1988. This vehicle belongs to the second batch which was painted in a simplified livery. Although the fleet has not done much beach roaming recently, having had a period in store, a full return to service is expected in 1997. *Geoff Rixon*

Introduction

The 'Heyday' series continues to expand, but this is the first to be devoted entirely to one type of bus. But then the Routemaster is no ordinary bus. It is famous the world over: through the tourists who visit London, the souvenir books and postcards, and the vehicles which have emigrated. In Britain it is the closest a particular bus is ever likely to get to becoming a household name.

How has this come to be? Well, I don't intend to start an argument over whether the Routemaster is the best bus ever built. In London alone, there are other claimants such as the 'B'-type, the RT or the RF. Clearly its fame is related to its longevity and this has to do with not just its quality but the fact that the Routemaster today represents the last motor bus of the traditional design which originated at the turn of the century. But the Routemaster is not just about nostalgia; the open platform bus with conductor is necessary for keeping London's traffic moving. The survivors of what is now a much depleted class are working as hard as they ever have, if not harder: a daily grind, Mondays to Saturdays, and yet they are between 29 and 38 years old. The Routemaster cannot realistically last for ever doing this punishing work, but a few more years certainly seem on the cards, given the body refurbishment and new engines which most have received. In addition, there is a fleet developing in Reading which is creating some excitement.

My interest in Routemasters began in 1956 when I worked for Weymann's in Addlestone, Surrey, and witnessed the completion of the only Weymann-bodied Routemaster, the Leyland-engined RML3. My admiration for the class grew over the years and I eventually formed an attachment to my local Showbus, Kingston garage's RM254, which is now my own pride and joy.

This album doesn't pretend to be a definitive history of the Routemaster, nor can it cover every possible variation, given a time span of 40 years and potentially 2,875 vehicles. Never has any other type of bus carried so many liveries, not even in London. The choice of material has, therefore, been rather subjective, but I have tried to balance the normal with the more unusual to provide some variety.

Acknowledgements

In compiling this title I would like to thank several photographers for supplying their colour slides, particularly the early material which is exceedingly hard to find. I am very grateful to James Whiting, Dick Riley, Roy Hobbs, John Aldridge, Steve Fennell, Trevor Saunders, D. T. Elliott, Gerald Mead, Mike Harries, Malcolm King, Dave Brown, Mike Harris, John May and Geoff Morant. Also, extreme thanks to Kevin McCormack, a past master at producing 'Heyday' books, for his many long hours of valuable assistance with photograph selection and text. As regards information and research, I was greatly assisted by Capital Transport's two Routemaster titles by Ken Blacker and their *Routemaster Handbook* by Andy Morgan.

I hope you will enjoy this pictorial tribute to a remarkable bus. Long may the Routemaster era continue!

Geoff Rixon
East Molesey, Surrey

First published 1997

ISBN 0 7110 2507 X

All rights reserved. No part of this book may be reproduced or transmitted in any form or by any means, electronic or mechanical, including photocopying, recording or by any information storage and retrieval system, without permission from the Publisher in writing.

© Geoff Rixon 1997

Published by Ian Allan Publishing

an imprint of Ian Allan Ltd, Terminal House, Station Approach, Shepperton, Surrey TW17 8AS. Printed by Ian Allan Printing Ltd, Coombelands House, Coombelands Lane, Addlestone, Surrey KT15 1HY

Above:

History in the Making

Unveiled to the public in October 1954 but not entering into service until February 1956, RM1 was over half-way through its initial proving trials when this rare colour view was taken at the Crystal Palace terminus of route 2 on 3 June 1956. Two months later this famous vehicle was back at Chiswick Works for modifications before re-entering service in March 1957. In fact, RM1's revenue-earning life lasted less than three years, although it earned its keep for a further 13 years on training duties. Sold and later repurchased by LT, RM1 is now preserved in running order. *R. C. Riley*

Right:

Wireless Operator

For just over six months in 1961, Sunday working of trolleybus route 609 produced the extraordinary sight of Routemasters operating alongside trolleybuses. This was to provide overtime opportunities at Highgate garage which had lost its trolleybuses whereas Finchley depot, the normal operator of the 609, retained its fleet until 7 November 1961. RM585 entered service in Highgate in February 1961 and was caught on camera at Moorgate. The vehicle was scrapped in 1985.
Trevor Saunders

Left:
Power Cut
Electric traction ceased at Hampton Court on 8 May 1962. Brand-new RMs 1130 and 1133 help to inaugurate the replacement bus service the following day. RM1133 now resides in France, but RM1130 was broken up.
Geoff Rixon

Above:
Birthplace
The famous production line at the AEC factory, Southall, in July 1962 finds RM1286 and RMC1460 in the final stages of preparation for delivery. Sadly, both these fine buses drew short straws, being scrapped 20 years later at Aldenham and Wombwell respectively. *Geoff Rixon*

7

Left:

Coach Routemaster Leyland

Numerically the last prototype RM, although actually delivered before RML3, had little in common with RMs 1–3. As well as being fitted out as a Green Line coach, it had an Eastern Coachworks body and, unlike the other prototypes which had very short working lives, RMC4, as it became, ran for over 20 years on normal duties. Entering service in October 1957, the vehicle is seen here in Walton Road, East Molesey in summer 1962 during the period of just over two years when it carried an experimental light green livery. Noteworthy features of this bus (which is still in working order today) are the three-piece front destination blind and the uniquely positioned offside route number box. *Geoff Rixon*

Above right:

Wot, No Paint!

In an attempt to emulate the unpainted Underground stock (in the days before graffiti) and also achieve a weight saving, LT ordered one Routemaster which, apart from certain moulded plastic parts, was in unpainted aluminium. Starting at Highgate on 13 July 1961, RM664 did the rounds of various garages and on its third anniversary entered service at Fulwell on route 285, on which it was operating when seen here at Heathrow in October 1964. By this time the vehicle was looking tarnished and after a total of four years in silver it was finally painted red. RM664 is now with South London while its original silver body is on RM577 in Reading. *Mike Harries*

Right:

Waiting for Take-off

The unique front-entranced RMF1254 spent four years in LT's fleet but ran only for other operators. Entering service in October 1962 in Liverpool, where it worked for a month, and then operating for two weeks in East Kent in March 1963, the vehicle found some continuity on the BEA Airline service from Gloucester Road, London, to Heathrow Airport, where it is seen in October 1964. Its success in operating with a luggage trailer sounded the death-knell for the 1½-deck coaches and resulted in the manufacture of 65 shorter BEA Routemasters. In November 1966, RMF1254 finally left London and spent the next 18 years with Northern General. The vehicle was then acquired for preservation. *Mike Harries*

Above:

Special Delivery

Only one operator outside London placed orders for the Routemaster. Northern General, seemingly influenced by the demonstrations given by RMF1254, took 50 similar vehicles. These were delivered between April 1964 and March 1965 and lasted a respectable 15 years in service. No 2091, in early livery, passes through Bishop Auckland Market Place in August 1965. In 1980 it was broken up, but several members of the fleet saw further use in various roles.

Geoff Morant

Right:

Short-lived Luxury

In 1962 a batch of 68 Routemaster coaches was introduced into Green Line service. More comfortable, spacious and faster than their bus counterparts, these coaches were intended to provide extra capacity on overloaded single-deck services, but arrived too late. Passenger traffic was by now declining and after only six years they were replaced by one-person-operated single-deckers and relegated to country bus work. RMC1500, which was re-registered in 1991 as ALC 368A and is now preserved, negotiates Marble Arch in August 1965. *Geoff Rixon*

Left:

Helping Out

In October 1965 19 red RMLs spent their first few weeks of service with the Country Department pending the setting up of comparative trials between RMLs and Atlanteans in the Central Area. All but two of the red RMLs went to Godstone where RML2287 was photographed. This bus still runs in London, in the ownership of Leaside Buses. *James Whiting*

Right:

Pursuit of Excellence

In the early days the Routemaster was constantly subject to modification and improvement in order to achieve perfection. Several efforts were made to obtain a practical and attractive radiator grille, culminating in the final version with the traditional triangle, pioneered by RMF1254. RM949 onwards were built with a stainless steel grille and matching central vertical strip whereas RM859, standing at Uxbridge in March 1966, features the earlier polished aluminium grille with red painted strip. Sold to Clydeside Scottish in 1986 and re-registered LDS 247A in 1990, this vehicle is now in Belgium. *James Whiting*

Above:

Family Connection

A Godstone garage Routemaster, just a few months old, meets AEC's previous 'blockbuster', the RT; in this case one in Green Line livery. RML2350 and RT4501 were photographed at Reigate Red Cross stand in June 1966. *Roy Hobbs*

Right:

Blue Triangle

RM1662 onwards were built with the final design of radiator grille incorporating the famous AEC/LT motif carried by previous generations of buses such as the RTs, STLs and LT/STs. Earlier RMs also received the later grille on overhaul. Cricklewood's RM1692, completed in October 1963, was still to receive its first overhaul when photographed at Golders Green station in September 1966. The vehicle was broken up in 1987. *James Whiting*

Splendid Isolation

Finding a rare gap in the traffic, six-month-old RM2130 negotiates the roundabout at Marble Arch in August 1965. By this time other design changes, apart from the revised radiator grille, had been made to the production models: the lower portion of the front ventilation grill was removed, thus enabling the cream band to be extended across the front of the bus and the brake cooling grilles in the front wings were blanked off. RM2130 went on to become a Shilibeer bus in 1979 and was broken up in 1987. *Geoff Rixon*

Uphill Task

The ascent to Epsom Downs from Epsom station was hard work for the fleet of heavily laden buses that operated the special Derby Day 406F service. RML2315, a lively two-year-old in this June 1967 photograph, has just reached the top. It is now running with Leaside Buses. *Roy Hobbs*

Left:

Discontinued Line

The last Routemaster to be built, RML2760, stands in Hyde Park on 19 May 1968 as part of a West End shopping promotion. Entering service at Upton Park on 1 March 1968, this vehicle is still at work today with Stagecoach East London, even wearing the same livery shown here. *John Aldridge*

Above:

Born Too Late

The rear-engined, one-person-operated Routemaster, FRM1, was the result of a joint venture between LT, AEC and Park Royal, planned in 1964. The vehicle entered service on 26 June 1967 at Tottenham garage but was beset by teething problems, including catching fire in August 1967. The view was taken a year later, after FRM1 had been returned to service and fitted with opening windows. Inevitably, by the time the vehicle had proved itself there were plenty of cheaper buses of similar design available which LT was required to purchase, leaving FRM1 as a one-off curiosity. *John Aldridge*

Above:

Flightmaster

With the introduction of larger aircraft in the 1960s, British European Airways needed to replace the fleet of 1½-deck coaches which transported passengers to Heathrow from the West London Air Terminal. Following the trials with RMF1254 towing a luggage trailer, BEA ordered 65 front-entranced Routemasters, the last standard-length models to be built. These were delivered between October 1966 and April 1967 and the service, which was operated by LT on behalf of BEA and, following the merger with BOAC, British Airways, lasted until 31 March 1979. In this view BEA No 41 is seen entering the Central Terminal Area at Heathrow in June 1969. Subsequently purchased by LT, it became RMA53 and was used as an Aldenham staff bus. It now resides at the Routemaster Heritage Centre in Hanwell, West London. *Mike Harries*

Right:

What an Insult!

The strangely named terminus of route 8 could well upset the sensitivities of a young AEC like RM2142, seen here moving shoppers in Oxford Street in July 1969. Completed in February 1965, this vehicle later became one of the Shilibeers in 1979 and was scrapped in 1992. *James Whiting*

Left:
Wheels Still Turning
Finsbury Square, near Liverpool Street, was the turn-round point for the 149 route, where RM688 is seen in August 1969. This standard RM, completed in April 1961, is one of the lucky survivors of the class. It still operates in London today, on London Central's route 36, working out of New Cross garage. *James Whiting*

Right:
Against the Odds
With the traditional red bus dominating London since the advent of LT in 1933 and the departure of the independents, any suggestion that one day multicoloured buses would take to the streets would have seemed laughable. This all changed in the early 1970s when 19 RMs and 7 RMLs received all-over advertisements. One of the most attractive was Hendon's RM786 with its horse racing theme. Seen at Childs Hill in March 1973, the vehicle eventually went to the knacker's yard in 1985. *James Whiting*

London and Manchester Assurance
406 Tolworth Stoneleigh Ewell Epsom
TADWORTH STATION
London and Manchester Assurance Your best man for life
RMC 1490
RG 81
London and Manchester Assurance
490 CLT

Left:

Decked Out

With all-over advertisement buses coming into vogue, London Country also decided to get in on the act. Unlike LT, the company decorated single- and double-deckers and the vehicles retained their liveries much longer. RMC1490 was one of three Routemasters so treated, its paintwork being only two months old when it was photographed at Kingston in May 1973. The vehicle survives today with Bluebird Buses of Perth. *James Whiting*

Above:

One in a Hundred

The Routemaster had very little in common with the Daimler Fleetline (DMS), but in the early 1970s some were turned out from Aldenham Works carrying the short-lived open roundel containing the words 'London Transport' which was worn by newly delivered DMS vehicles. Before the gold fleetname returned (briefly), RM1385 was photographed at Victoria in July 1973. The bus was broken up in 1989. *R. C. Riley*

Above:

Life-size Model

RM952 was one Dinky toy which could not be bought over the counter. Initially allocated in this livery to Walworth garage for use on route 12, the vehicle spent its first few days working route 45. Here it is in August 1973 at Stockwell station, the fading light enhanced by flash. Thirteen years later, it was reduced to scrap.
Steve Fennell

Right:

Brightness Control

Yet another multicoloured Routemaster was RM682 which advertised PYE, the electronics company, for seven months. Standing rather appropriately outside the BBC's Bush House at Aldwych in October 1973, RM682 was sold in 1988 to United Counties, becoming No 703 in their fleet. Re-registered HVS 937 in 1992, it is currently in storage. *D. T. Elliott*

Left:
Last Coach
A total of 112 Routemaster coaches were built for Green Line Services. Here is the final vehicle dating from July 1965 seen leaving Crawley bus station in June 1975, following demotion to bus work, and transfer to London Country. Saved from the scrap yard by LT in 1979, it was initially used for driver training before being fully refurbished for use on route 149 operating from Edmonton garage, where it was also their Showbus. RCL2260 is still in active service working for London Coaches from Wandsworth garage on sightseeing and private hire work. *John May*

Above:
Floral Bonnet
All-over advertising provided plenty of scope for artistic licence, although the connection between flowers and heating engineers is a trifle obscure. With a backdrop which seems to be a permanent feature of London, RML2280 is seen near Mansion House in June 1975. This was one of five RMLs to receive the full treatment and along with RM1196, which carried the same livery, was the last to run as part of this advertising campaign, which spanned nearly seven years. RML2280 is still at work in London, with Leaside Buses. *R. C. Riley*

Below:

Distant Cousins

Two AECs with very different reputations stand at Staines West station in September 1975. RMs operated route 117 for 16 years until January 1978 and RM1281 remained at Hounslow garage until 1987, when it was withdrawn and scrapped. *R. C. Riley*

Right:

Green Line Survivor

At a time when most RCLs had been relegated to bus work and repainted in National Bus Company leaf green, RCL2226 remained in traditional Green Line livery for operation on the last crew-operated coach service, route 709, which was not converted to OBO until May 1976. Eight months earlier, RCL2226 was photographed at South Croydon. Dispatched to the breaker's yard in March 1979, the vehicle survived through being repurchased by LT and was put to work on route 149. It was sold by LT in 1985 and now serves as a catering vehicle for a film company. *R. C. Riley*

Above:

Weirdsider

This would be a more appropriate term for Northern General No 3069, whose official name was Wearsider. Previously numbered 2085, the vehicle received serious front-end damage in 1972 (which some may say it still has in this photograph!). Rather than writing off the bus, the company rebuilt it for one-person-operation by moving back the driver's position. Unpopular with staff, its use was intermittent and no other RMs were modified. Displaying 'Pay as you enter' signage, No 3069 picks up at Washington New Town in August 1976. Two years later the bus ceased to exist. *Steve Fennell*

Right:

Coming into Leaf

As a National Bus Company subsidiary London Country was later obliged to adopt the corporate pale green colours when vehicles required repainting. RMCs started to receive this livery from July 1973 and in this example RMC1465, operating out of Swanley garage in October 1975 on route 423, is photographed in the picturesque village of Farningham in Kent. By 1978 the bus was repurchased by LT but never used, going to the breaker's yard two years later.
Steve Fennell

Left:
Monarch of the Road
When the all-over advertisement craze ended, another departure from red livery was soon to appear. To celebrate HM The Queen's Silver Jubilee in 1977, 25 recently overhauled Routemasters were painted silver and renumbered SRM1–25. Sponsored by various companies, the selected vehicles ran from February to November 1977 and SRM25 (RM1850) was caught on camera in June travelling along New Oxford Street. Nine years later it was sold to Clydeside Scottish and broken up for spares. *Dave Brown*

Above:
Spray Booth
With generous application of masking material, this unidentified Routemaster is in the course of receiving a first-class paint job at Aldenham Works in March 1978. *Steve Fennell*

Above:

Forced Landing

The third and final livery carried by the Routemasters used on the airline service is seen on No 55 at Heathrow Airport in March 1978. By this time, only 38 of the former 65-strong fleet were still operating and a year later the remainder were grounded when the service was withdrawn. After being renumbered RMA58, the vehicle spent eight years as a staff bus; it then enjoyed a further spell in public service, first with Verwood Transport of Poole, Dorset, then Blue Triangle of Bootle, and finally MTL Merseybus. Repaired following an accident in 1995, the vehicle has been repainted in Liverpool Corporation green and cream livery for the local Heritage service. *Geoff Rixon*

Right:

Going to the Zoo

In the days when Chessington was renowned for animals rather than for white-knuckle rides, the 65 route ran all the way through from Ealing instead of terminating as it does now at Kingston. In October 1978, Norbiton's RM1321 (now preserved) passes through leafy Surbiton, wearing the long-lived solid white roundels which Routemasters received upon overhaul from 1974 onwards. *Geoff Rixon*

Left:
Omnibus Celebration
George Shilibeer gave London its first regular bus service in 1829. To commemorate the 150th anniversary, a dozen Routemasters, numbered between 2130 and 2208, were painted in the original Shilibeer colours which many regard as the most attractive livery worn by this class. Each bus was sponsored by advertisers and moved between garages every three months. RM2191 was based at Hammersmith when it was photographed rounding Trafalgar Square on 13 May 1979. The vehicle lasted until 1989. *Geoff Rixon*

Above:
Special Identity
The 1,000th Routemaster was completed in October 1961 and was notable for being the only one of the first 1,600 in the class not to carry a registration containing the letters 'LT'. This view of RM1000 was taken in Hampstead Road, near Euston station, in April 1980 when the vehicle was based at Clapton garage. Later that year it received a full overhaul at Aldenham Works and became Croydon's Showbus. RM1000 has happily survived into preservation. *Geoff Rixon*

Left:

Brush-off

Painted up in 1979 as an all-over advertisement to celebrate 200 years of Wisdom toothbrushes, RM1237 followed a planned programme of working out of several London garages, including Palmers Green, from which it was operating when photographed at Mornington Crescent in April 1980. Unfortunately, its celebrity status was short-lived because it was withdrawn in November 1982 and broken up shortly after. *Geoff Rixon*

Above:

Feeling the Heat

The first 253 Routemaster bodies had non-opening upper-deck front windows, but the lack of adequate ventilation resulted in opening windows becoming standard. After overhaul, many early bodies were fitted to later chassis, but RM15, seen here leaving Victoria station in June 1978, has the correct type of body. Re-registered KGH 602A in 1989, this fine vehicle was broken up in 1992. *Geoff Rixon*

Above:

Odd Man Out

These three RMLs standing at Brent Cross in July 1980 might all look the same, but RML2324, nearest to the camera, is third-hand. Originally delivered in green livery to LT's Country Area in 1965, this bus was transferred to London Country on the latter's formation in 1970 and was bought back by LT in 1979 for Central Area service. It now operates with South London. *Geoff Rixon*

Right:

Sales Resistance

1979 not only brought the Shilibeer livery but also the striking red and yellow Shoplinker colours. These were carried by 16 Routemasters working out of Stockwell garage which plied between Marble Arch and the various West End stores which sponsored the service. Starting on 7 April 1979 (a sad day for RT enthusiasts), the Shoplinkers ran throughout the summer, but insufficient patronage brought about their demise at the end of September. RM2189, seen here in Oxford Street in June, survived at Stockwell until 1993 when it was withdrawn for scrap. *Dave Brown*

43

Above:

Sunday Best

Clapton's RM1568 looks in fine condition as it saunters along Old Street, Shoreditch, on 10 August 1980, during the days of Sunday closing. Shopping habits may have changed now, but RM1568 soldiers on at the time of writing. In its 33rd year of London service and still retaining its original registration, this Routemaster belongs to MTL, operating out of Holloway garage. *Geoff Rixon*

Right:

Revamped in Red

The once resplendent Green Line Routemaster coaches were becoming very shabby by the late 1970s, but once repurchased by LT, 40 RCLs were renovated for further passenger service. Platform doors, twin headlamps and luggage racks were removed, interiors were retrimmed in DMS-style dark blue moquette and the buses repainted red. Looking magnificent and still retaining their larger engines, they ousted fleetlines from route 149 on 10 August 1980, working from Stamford Hill garage. RCL2256, seen here in Kingsland Road, was later to suffer rear end damage and was rebuilt with a standard RM platform. The RCLs were displaced in late 1984 and RCL2256 became Southend Transport No 121. It is currently in the hands of a dealer. *Geoff Rixon*

Left:
Lending a Hand
The conductor of heavily laden RM1831 helps the driver cross the traffic flow at Hyde Park Corner as the Dalston-based vehicle turns into Knightsbridge in April 1981. Within a few years this bus had been cut up. *Geoff Rixon*

Below:
Hard Day's Work
The relaxed retirement lifestyle of the prototype Routemaster coach, the only RM to be retained by London Country, was sometimes disturbed in the early 1980s by some active duty. One such occasion was on Saturday 20 June 1981 when RMC4, formerly CRL4, worked special relief journeys on Green Line route 719 to mark the retirement of Garston garage's last conductress. The vehicle is seen at Marble Arch battling its way to Victoria. *Geoff Rixon*

Left:

Slow Coach

The once familiar sight of Routemaster coaches in their splendid two-tone green livery traversing London had long ceased by the time LT repurchased these vehicles from London Country in 1979/80. Most were in poor external condition following years of country bus work and it was a treat when examples like RMC1515 were repainted in London bus red. Alas, there was little suitable work for these vehicles and many were destined to plod around London on learner duties. RMC1515, seen here in April 1981 at Hyde Park Corner, was converted to open-top in 1987 and is now in store. *Geoff Rixon*

Above:

Parcel Bus

The marriage of HRH Prince Charles and Lady Diana Spencer on 28 July 1981 provided another excuse to repaint Routemasters in a special livery. Eight recently overhauled vehicles from Aldenham Works were decorated with painted silver ribbons and bows and carried a large telegram painted on the offside rear panels with a message from the advertising sponsors. These buses ran from 13 June until the autumn and this view in Whitehall taken the day before the wedding depicts RM534 from Hammersmith (Riverside) garage working a one-day special service to view the decorations. RM534 departed this world in 1985. *Geoff Rixon*

Above:

Winter Wonderland

Heavy overnight snow gives way to a cold sunny morning as Palmers Green's RM1928 adorns this Christmas card scene at Muswell Hill in December 1981. The vehicle was broken up in 1988. *Dave Brown*

Right:

Timewarp

The Showbus era was getting into full swing with competition hotting up between garages when one of the finest examples was captured at Heathrow Airport in January 1982. Apart from the absence of rear wheel discs ('dustbin lids') apparently for safety reasons, Harrow Weald's RM737 is seen in full 1960s condition and was proudly displayed by LT staff at rallies when not in service. It is now in private hands and still attends shows. *Geoff Rixon*

Left:

Forest Ranger

This was the name given to RM2116 by Seven Kings garage in 1983 and is still carried today in preservation. The christening coincided with its repainting into 1933 livery for LT's Golden Jubilee, but back in June 1982 RM2116 was just another Routemaster in standard livery, proceeding along South Street, Romford.
Dave Brown

Above:

Final Tour of Duty

FRM1 had a chequered career which ended with a six-year stint on the Round London Sightseeing Tour. In July 1982, during its last summer of public service, this unique vehicle was photographed at Marble Arch. Eighteen months earlier it had been repainted into original livery, apart from the repositioning of the front bullseye due to the fitting of an air intake. FRM1 was delicensed on 3 February 1983 and handed over to the LT museum. *Geoff Rixon*

Above:

Green Street Red

With Routemaster operation now confined to Central London, it is easy to forget that red RMs used to penetrate the countryside around the capital. In the case of Bromley garage's route 261, Routemasters ran for only seven months and in March 1983 RM1079 was caught on camera at the curiously named Green Street Green. Five years later, the vehicle succumbed to the breaker's torch. *Geoff Rixon*

Right:

Capital Gold

To celebrate LT's Golden Jubilee in 1983, Aldenham Works amazed the bus world by producing an all-gold RM. Seen on its first day of service (30 April 1983) turning into Thornton Heath garage, the aptly numbered RM1983 worked from several garages until it was returned to red in February 1984. The following year it was sold to Kelvin Scottish and is now in store with Stagecoach Cumberland at Whitehaven. *Geoff Rixon*

Left:

Heading for Reading

In its original guise, RM993 is seen sweeping round Hyde Park Corner on 28 July 1983. Fresh from overhaul at Aldenham and still without advertisements, the vehicle is working from Willesden garage. In 1988 it left for Southend, becoming No 107, but returned once to operate route 111 for the 1993 Hounslow garage open day, proudly wearing its blue and white livery. Today this bus is No 2 in Reading Mainline's fleet. *Geoff Rixon*

Above:

Last Anniversary

Four garages decided to commemorate LT's Golden Jubilee by each painting one of its Routemasters in 1933 livery. Chalk Farm was fortunate in having RM1933 itself and on 18 August 1983 it was photographed under the watchful eye of one of the Trafalgar Square lions. The subsequent dismemberment of LT has brought an end to further anniversaries, but RM1933 lives on (see page 67). *Geoff Rixon*

Shoppers' Express

A surprising development in late 1983 was the introduction of Routemaster-operated limited stop routes in the Kingston area. Unfortunately, passenger loadings failed to reach expectations and the services lasted barely a year. Kingston garage's Showbus RM254 brings a touch of class to the K2 at Berrylands in April 1984. By this time the services were operating from Norbiton garage following Kingston's closure in January 1984. Withdrawn in August 1985, this fine vehicle is now the author's indulgence. *Geoff Rixon*

Rover's Return

This April 1984 view shows Putney's RM104 crossing Roehampton Common on route 74. Today, the bus can be found on BTS-operated route 13. Nothing strange about that, you may think, except that in the intervening years RM104 travelled 400 miles to work for Clydeside Scottish, who re-registered it as LDS 280A, and then spent three years with Southend Transport. No one would have predicted that it would operate again in London. *Geoff Rixon*

Left:

Multicolour Revival

All-over advertising returned to London in 1984 when three RMLs were duly decorated. The choice was between Underwoods or underwear. RML2492, seen here in Whitehall, was the lucky one of the trio, advertising chemists rather than men's pants. It is now with London Central. *Geoff Rixon*

Above:

Deceptive Appearances

What purports to be an early photograph of the first production Routemaster, RM5, which entered service in June 1959, is an illusion. RM8 was actually built six months before RM5, even though it did not enter service for nearly 18 years; also, RM5 was built with non-opening upper-deck front windows and has, therefore, lost its original body. This view, at the pigeon end of Whitehall, was in fact taken in August 1984 at a time when the vehicle was a Showbus. It is still in London today, working alongside 94 RMLs as Leaside Buses' only standard Routemaster. *Geoff Rixon*

61

Above:

Water Works

Chiswick was renowned for its skid pan and during the 1984 open day spectators were able to watch RM1740 perform. The works, which opened in 1922, are now razed to the ground, but the bus lives on in Uruguay. *Geoff Rixon*

Right:

Sun Worshipper

These days RM395 basks in California rather than Mitcham. Back in October 1984 it was working from Merton garage and displays its new extended offside advertising panel. *Geoff Rixon*

Left:

Topless 20

A total of 39 RMs and 11 RCLs were overhauled at Aldenham in 1986 for the new 'Original London Transport Sightseeing Tour' and 20 of the RMs had their roofs removed. All were repainted in traditional LT livery and fitted with public address systems. This view shows open-top RMs 94 and 80 at the Houses of Parliament in June 1986. Both vehicles have since been extended to over 32ft with the addition of a full-size window bay and are now designated ERMs. *Geoff Rixon*

Above:

Route Branding

In spring 1986 an eyecatching livery was introduced to promote the No 15 service, consisting of yellow roofs and waistbands and large route posters. The roofs were quickly repainted, but RML2402, seen in June 1986 outside the Law Courts in the Strand, displays the double yellow bands. *Geoff Rixon*

Left:
Invasion of Scotland
1986 was a year of widespread Routemaster withdrawals in London and a new market for these old stalwarts opened up across the border. Some 200 Routemasters made the journey to Scotland, including RM37, seen here enjoying the evening sunshine near Paisley while working Clydeside's route 613 in July 1986. Re-registered LDS 173A in 1989, the vehicle was scrapped the following year. *Geoff Rixon*

Right:
Forgotten Hero
In 1983 RM1933 was one of four Routemasters selected to carry a special livery to celebrate LT's Golden Jubilee (see page 57). Three years later the vehicle was just another RM surplus to LT's requirements and fortunate to find a buyer who was not a scrap merchant. Sporting Kelvin Scottish's yellow and blue livery, RM1933 was photographed on the outskirts of Glasgow in April 1987. Within a few months it was up for sale again, once more escaping the scrapyard and ending up with Stagecoach Cumberland at Whitehaven, where it is currently in store. *Geoff Rixon*

Above:

Conductors in Corby

One of the Stagecoach group subsidiaries, United Counties, took delivery of a fleet of RMs at the beginning of 1988 for operation in Bedford and Corby, making full use of the Routemaster name. RM980, seen here at Corby in May 1988, moved on to another Stagecoach company, East Midland, in the following year and received a new registration, USK 625. The vehicle is currently with Bluebird Buses in Perth. *Geoff Rixon*

Right:

Generals on Parade

Two RMs, 89 and 1590, were painted in the style of livery used until 1933 by the London General Omnibus Company. This was to celebrate the launch of the new London General Company in April 1989. On 6 May, purely by chance as a result of traffic congestion which caused one of these RMs to undertake an unexpected short journey, both buses arrived together at Victoria station where this view was taken. RM89 was sold in 1994 to McGills Bus Service, Barrhead, who re-registered it as VYJ 893. RM1590 belongs to a medical charity in Ashford, Middlesex. *Geoff Rixon*

Left:

Beach Buggy

After borrowing vehicles to evaluate the reintroduction of crew operation, Southend Transport took the plunge and acquired their first Routemasters in 1988. Shortly after entry into service, RM1061 is seen at Belgrave Road, Eastwood. Following a change in the company's ownership, RM operation fell from favour and RM1061 moved to another coast, crossing the pond in the process. It now belongs to the Beach Bus Company in Kittyhawk, North Carolina, and has been converted to open-top. *Steve Fennell*

Right:

RMC Revival

Whereas the RCLs had a short-lived renaissance in the early 1980s while the RMCs were in the doldrums, the tables turned in 1989 when half a dozen RMCs were painted red with gold window surrounds and waistband. This was for the new X15 service from East London to the West End, on which the resplendent RMC1461 was photographed at East Beckton on 26 May 1989. This vehicle is now operated by Stagecoach East London and carries full Green Line livery, while two other RMCs have retained their red and gold. They can be seen today on route 15. *Mike Harris*

Above:

Triple Cream

Designed for a single cream band, RM364 nevertheless looks very smart in East Yorkshire's traditional livery of dark blue relieved with three cream bands. All that is missing is the Beverley Bar domed roof! Following the success of its first Routemaster service introduced in April 1988, East Yorkshire bought a further batch of RMs, this time from Clydeside Scottish. Alas, crew operations lasted only a few months and just before cessation RM364 was photographed at Ormond Park Estate. *Steve Fennell*

Right:

Changing Appearance

Former LT red RM1183 operated from London and Country's Leatherhead garage in three different liveries during its two-year stint there between 1993 and 1995. The vehicle arrived in Southend Transport blue and white, initially on loan to cover a temporary vehicle shortage, and entered service in this livery. It then received standard London and Country colours as recorded here at Ewell Village when working route 406. Finally, it was repainted in former LT Lincoln green — the first standard length Routemaster bus to operate in this livery. RM1183 was sold to Nostalgiabus in 1996. *Steve Fennell*

Left:

Dead Ringer

Looking remarkably like a Brighton, Hove & District bus, RM1361 was one of 27 Routemasters with new Iveco engines which were painted red and cream by South London for route 159. Re-registered VYJ 808 in 1993, the vehicle is seen heading from Whitehall into Parliament Square in July 1994 wearing its final style of bullseye. South London was acquired by the Cowie Group in December 1994. *Geoff Rixon*

Above:

Lucky for Some

Under the tendering arrangements route 13 from Golders Green to Aldwych was awarded to BTS of Borehamwood, Hertfordshire, in 1993 and the company inherited 22 RMLs for this service. Displaying the BTS orange/red livery with yellow waistband and route diagram maps is newly painted RML2538, photographed in June 1994. The vehicle is standing at the rare mid-1930s tubular bus shelter beside St Martin-in-the-Fields, adjacent to Trafalgar Square. *Gerald Mead*

Left:
Brief Blossoming
White Rose coaches of Glasshoughton, Yorkshire, purchased five Iveco-engined RMs in 1994 for use between Leeds and Castleford. Alas, this was another short-lived Routemaster service, lasting only six months. This shot, taken just before cessation in May 1995, shows RM395 on route 164 at Cross Gates, Leeds, its appearance marred by an unfortunate blind display. Four of the White Rose vehicles, including RM395, have since emigrated to America where they have been converted to open-top. *Malcolm King*

Right:
Life Begins at 40
In 1996 the Routemasters clocked up 40 years of service in London. Although the fleet has been decimated, this is not apparent to the casual observer in the main streets of the West End, which are still filled with Routemasters from Mondays to Saturdays. However, the buses are mostly RMLs and there are only about 100 standard RMs left, operating mainly on routes 36, 139 and 159. In June 1996 RM268, 36 years young and still carrying its original registration, has just been freshly painted by its owners, MTL London, in this Regent Street view. *Dave Brown*

Left:
Unusual Pick-me-up
RMC1510 is certainly a tonic for any fresh-air fiends who want to travel on what is currently London's only open-topper operating a normal route. Centrewest operate a large fleet of RMLs from Middle Row garage and also have this solitary ex-Green Line coach. Its roof was removed in 1989 and it is the only RMC to have a Cummins engine (ex-RM2033). This view was taken at Oxford Circus in June 1996. *Geoff Rixon*

Above:

Big Hoppa

Contrasting with the current generation of Hoppa midibuses is ERM94, one of 10 RMs lengthened in 1990 by the addition of a full window bay in the centre of the bus. Photographed in July 1996 in Whitehall, the vehicle can be seen in a previous incarnation on page 64. *Geoff Rixon*

Right:

Going West

While the numerous fleets of second-hand Routemasters have all but vanished, a remarkable expansion is under way some 35 miles west of London. In Reading an adventurous company trading as Reading Mainline has, since 1994, been gathering up AEC-engined RMs, which now number around 30, and is looking for more. Two examples, ex-RM180 (No 20) and ex-RM172 (No 10) meet on Route E in July 1996. No 10 was once Southend Transport's Showbus, as evidenced by the offside route indicator box. *Geoff Rixon*

Road transport colour books from IAN ALLAN Publishing

British Lorries in Colour
By S. W. Stevens-Stratten   ISBN: 0711022453   7.25in x 9.5in   H/B   **£11.99**

Bus Scene in Colour: Ten Years of Deregulation
By Stephen Morris   ISBN: 0711024936   7.25in x 9.5in   H/B   **£11.99**

The Heyday of the British Lorry: Historic Commercial Vehicles in Colour
By Malcolm Broad & Peter Durham   ISBN: 0711023867   7.25in x 9.5in   H/B   **£10.99**

The Heyday of the Classic Coach
By Kevin Lane   ISBN: 0711022704   7.25in x 9.5in   H/B   **£11.99**

The Heyday of the London Bus — 3
By Kevin McCormack   ISBN: 0711024863
7.25in x 9.5in   H/B   **£11.99**

The Heyday of the Traction Engine
By Eric Sawford   ISBN: 071102362X   7.25in x 9.5in   H/B   **£10.99**

The Heyday of the Tram — 2
By Peter Waller   ISBN: 0711023964   7.25in x 9.5in   H/B   **£11.99**

The Heyday of the Trolleybus — 2
By Geoff Lumb   ISBN: 0711024634   7.25in x 9.5in   H/B   **£11.99**

Tractors in Colour
By Alan C. Butcher   ISBN: 0711022461   7.25in x 9.5in   H/B   **£11.99**

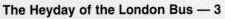

HOW TO ORDER: Simply call **LITTLEHAMPTON BOOK SERVICES** on **01903 736736**, quoting reference code **BART1**, your credit card details and the ISBN of the book(s) required. Alternatively, write to: **IAN ALLAN MAIL ORDER, Dept BART1, 10-14 Eldon Way, Lineside Estate, Littlehampton, West Sussex BN17 7HE. Fax: 01903 730914. (Please add £2.50 post & packing charges UK, £3.60 overseas.)**

For further information on Ian Allan Publishing/Dial House titles, please contact: The Marketing Department on **01932 855909.** For a copy of our latest Books and Videos Catalogue please write to: The Marketing Department, Ian Allan Ltd, Coombelands House, Coombelands Lane, Addlestone, Surrey KT15 1HY. Please include an A5 sae to the value of 40p.